WHAT SMALL SOUND

WHAT SMALL SOUND

poems

Francesca Bell

Red Hen Press | *Pasadena, CA*

Book design by Shelby Wallace

Library of Congress Cataloging-in-Publication Data

Names: Bell, Francesca, 1967– author.
Title: What small sound: poems / Francesca Bell.
Description: First edition. | Pasadena, CA: Red Hen Press, [2023]
Identifiers: LCCN 2022027777 (print) | LCCN 2022027778 (ebook) | ISBN
    9781636280790 (hardcover) | ISBN 9781636281018 (paperback) | ISBN
    9781636280806 (ebook)
Subjects: LCGFT: Poetry.
Classification: LCC PS3602.E4528 W58 2023 (print) | LCC PS3602.E4528
    (ebook) | DDC 811/.6—dc23/eng/20220616
LC record available at https://lccn.loc.gov/2022027777
LC ebook record available at https://lccn.loc.gov/2022027778

The National Endowment for the Arts, the Los Angeles County Arts Commission, the Ahmanson
Foundation, the Dwight Stuart Youth Fund, the Max Factor Family Foundation, the Pasadena
Tournament of Roses Foundation, the Pasadena Arts & Culture Commission and the City of
Pasadena Cultural Affairs Division, the City of Los Angeles Department of Cultural Affairs,
the Audrey & Sydney Irmas Charitable Foundation, the Meta & George Rosenberg Foundation,
the Albert and Elaine Borchard Foundation, the Adams Family Foundation, Amazon Literary
Partnership, the Sam Francis Foundation, and the Mara W. Breech Foundation partially support
Red Hen Press.

First Edition
Published by Red Hen Press
www.redhen.org

JUN 1 3 2023

Acknowledgments

Grateful acknowledgment is made to the editors of the following publications where these poems first appeared, sometimes in different versions:

Afrikana.ng: "Sorrow Is Innate in the Human"; *Blackbird*: "Intention Tremor," "The Way Some People Laugh at Funerals"; *Blue Lyra Review*: "Burdens"; *B O D Y*: "Admissions," "How Like a God," "Manifest Image," "Perimenopause," "Preferred Pronouns: We/Us/ Ours," "Turning a Corner"; *burntdistrict*: "Domestic Failings," "Jubilations"; *Connotation Press*: "Hush," "Menopause, Insomnia, News"; *5 AM*: "Instrument Left in Its Case," "Maybe Stillness Saves Us After All"; *Flycatcher*: "I Leave My Window Open Now to Hear Them," "The Sound When the Held Note Ceases"; *GARGOYLE*: "Endometrial Biopsy," "Going to the Sperm Bank"; *Mom Egg Review*: "Proofs"; *Mount Hope*: "Love Is a Song You Listen to Later"; *NELLE*: "Deciduous," "Dusk, the Day I Drove My Child to the Partial Hospitalization Program," "Mistakes of One Kind," "The Dentist Says It's from Some Earlier Damage"; *New Ohio Review*: "Just Like All the Girls"; *Nimrod*: "Learning to Love the World That Is," "Like a Friend," "Making You Noise"; *Passages North*: "Scorpions"; *Pedestal*: "Lessons," "Lightning Coming Closer All the Time"; *Pirene's Fountain*: "Rhubarb," "Two Stories"; *Quiddity*: "Empty," "My Daughter Was Always the Resourceful One"; *Rattle*: "Containment," "*Girlfriend of Las Vegas Gunman Says Her Fingerprints Would Likely Be on Ammo*," "Late Mammogram," "Love in the Time of Covid-19," "What Small Sound," "Where We Are Most Tender"; *Red Wheelbarrow*: "Swimming the Flambeau"; *RHINO*: "How Destruction Comes to Look Like Possibility"; *Salamander*: "One Day, My Body"; *Slipstream*: "Breaking Eggs," "Why I Don't Drink"; *South Dakota Review*: "What Did I Know"; *Spillway*: "Tutor"; *Tar River Poetry*: "Late Blooming," "Right to Life"; *Thalia*: "Taking Your Place"; and *The Charlotte Poetry Review*: "From the Beginning."

My deepest thanks to readers, first and last, for receiving my poems. And to my friends and family, present and past, for loving me.

for my mother, who made the path I walked into the world

Contents

I

Jubilations

Every two minutes, an American woman is raped,
her body forced open in the time it takes me to tear
this organic tomato to its pulpy center and bite in,
letting juice run down my chin, stinging.

This tomato a celebration on my tongue reminding me
of the night we spent six hundred dollars on dinner for two,
as that man in Colorado loaded guns into his car.

Food arrived on silk pillows: tiny, purple carrots,
radishes like marbles—fairy vegetables—and a miniature,
individual loaf of bread for each course, and each course
with its own silverware and army of people washing in the back.

As we clinked our glasses together,
he checked his ammunition and gas mask,
and people wondered, *popcorn or candy*.

This morning, I ran through a forest kept tidy
by rich people like me, Eminem shuffling smoothly
through my iPhone. Somewhere in China,
a young man folded his ruined hands in his lap.

My palms were raised, open. I imagined texting
prayers straight to Heaven: *OMG. OMG.*
Thank You for this world of green grass and suffering.

Learning to Love the World That Is

It's good to walk this first smokeless morning
in weeks. Though fires burn not so far away,
winds are favorable, at the moment, to me.
I hum as I pass the twenty-three RVs of the unhoused
lined up neatly along the road, a smattering of tents,
the tarped and trailered boat someone lives in.
As if it were a camp and not an encampment.
I'm thinking of rain, which is not forecast,
and hate, which definitely is, and a restaurant
I loved that incinerated last week.
The flight of steps to the entrance survived,
and at the top hangs the missing space
where we celebrated our twentieth anniversary
in style. Joggers pass me, and I notice how,
though we cover our faces,
we cannot paper over the losses
of this strange year. *Miserly world,*
I think, just as flock after flock of geese
lift their generous bodies
from the stinking slough and fly low
over the trees I walk among.
They are like a book God writes
across this autumn sky, its pages fluttering.
The very God who inscribes Himself
on the hills' dry faces, who etches suffering
onto a world that scorches,
its forests immolating and magnificent.
So like the chef at Meadowood who shattered
dishes and people just before he plated beauty.
I'm like a person who resists at first
the temptation of a kiss but then leans fully in,
my heart rising on the voices of the geese,
their cry a hinge that sings as it does
the necessary work of opening.

Two Stories

In the dream, Mother, we live in two stories
near a field parched white, and you know
the field will come alive with fire,
and fire will flicker to our house
and consume it completely. Yet you say
I may not go up the stairs and bring out
my boxes of poems or carry my cat
with gold eyes from the treacherous
rooms. You refuse to help me carry
my books or pictures of me at every age
or the painting of the red-haired girl praying.
I run fast as I can to each house, begging
for someone to help me save what I have saved
of the years of my life. But no one moves
fast enough. So I come to stand with you,
Mother, and watch as our house lights up,
a blaze dancing through every room.
I must stand there knowing
each green plant I have watered folds
in on itself, and my face in the photograph
of my fourth birthday blisters and weeps
down the page. I must listen and clearly hear
my own voice, my poems hissing in the flames.

Making You Noise

for my mother

The day before you go deaf completely,
I will make you noise.
I will bring birds, bracelets,
chimes to hang in wind.
We will drive from Idaho
to Washington again,
and I will read to keep you
awake. I will tap
little poems on the backs
of your arms and neck
to be sure you hear me.
I will play spoons on your body
in restaurants, smack my lips,
heave you sighs,
each one deeper than the last.
We will finally shout.
And then, as quiet
slips in, settling over,
I will speak. I will keep speaking.
I will sing you nonsense songs
until you sleep.

Domestic Failings

Do not envy the pancake turner
its plain shape, undistorted by heat,

or the slotted spoon
its talent for distillation.

Accept your plates,
their generous, blank-slate faces,

and the fact you'll never match
your Tupperware's discretion.

The pizza wheel effortlessly divvies.
Learn its clean lines, its appetite for separation.

Note the trash compactor's concision,
the iron's easy way with the agitated

knowing you can't compare
to even the kitchen chair—

its stolid, dependable shape,
its immutable spine.

Empty

Those broken winter midnights, the baby's wailing having woken me,
her stutter-stopping cries made a song we rocked to, nursing.

She was always sick then, her ear's tiny drum bursting bloody
on the pillow, her breath ragged as a ripped seam against my areola.

She labored all night like a woman who tries to bring the terrible miracle
forth. My breasts are grown useless now, but still I haul them around

as I carried that girl on my hip well past when she could walk,
a weight that shifted my bones out of place. These nights,

spine still off-kilter, my body does not settle. Her mind
now is murky, my grown girl, like sediment stirred up.

I hear her in the dark hurling objects into her piled-high pillows,
crying, and I lie, O, I lie with nothing left to offer her.

Maybe Stillness Saves Us After All

The sight of her terrifies:
reaching, articulate legs,
dark, hairy body,
but I allow her anyway—
size of a slow hand—
to move across me.
She lifts each leg like a dancer
before placing the iridescent pads
of her feet on my bare skin.

Her touch is softer
than any human's,
softer than the first kiss
of a shy boy, or the fluttering breath
of my babies when I lean in close
to check them. If I am quiet,
she keeps her fangs
tucked up, and I am a floor,
just something to cross.

Maybe all my fears are like this,
creeping carefully over me
as my lips stumble
to navigate hurried prayers.
If I am still and do not start,
perhaps calamity will pass,
as the tarantula does,
on the way to somewhere else.

Late Blooming

Mid-January, and still
the last amaryllis refuses.
Planted in October,
it just now raises
a green bud tip
to the bright window.
Inside the plain package
waits a blaring red,
the flower furled,
held like breath
in the trumpeter's body.

Instrument Left in Its Case

My life sucks, but my wife won't,
he said, rolling onto his back
on my massage table.

He laughed, a painful choke,
as his penis slowly rose,
quiet question tenting
the flannel sheet.

I think he wanted—
not to be *blown*,
but played,

trapped song
coaxed from him
by careful embouchure
and another's breath.

I heard the faint thrum
of his loneliness
all the way home.

I Leave My Window Open Now to Hear Them

Nights, I hear barn owls calling,
shrill as hunger stripped bare—
and think of the onion farmer
from east of the mountains, his broad,
exhausted body on my massage table,
the owl he told me screamed
all winter from his barn rafters.
He said the sound made the cold
colder when he trudged
from field to barn to house.

After I touched all the places
I was licensed to—bunched,
tender shoulders that crept
toward his ears; beat-up hands,
leathery as a dog's paw pads;
each buttock's lonely
hillock giving gently
beneath my forearm's strokes—
he sat up and asked
if I'd have sex with him.

He promised not to hurt me,
to buy me dinner after.
He said it plain, did not look away.
But I was twenty and knew nothing
of desolation, or owls,
or wintering-over onions,
or of a farmer pacing ugly acres,
as layer upon layer of stinging,
weeping sweetness forms
beneath the frozen-solid ground.

From the Beginning

I see you rise like an apparition
when the doctor waves his wand
across my belly. I see your face.
You turn toward me
the orbs of your eyes: dark,
impenetrable. Your arms move,
a thrashing like running or swimming,
and I see hands unfurl at the ends
of them. Hands that will hold on
and let go. Your feet already
walk you across the slick carpet
of my insides. Onscreen, they glimmer
like ghost feet taking you places I cannot.
From the beginning, I know you
are leaving. Chilled in my flimsy gown
in the dim room, I watch the swell
of me, bare and glistening,
under which you move.
The screen is lit with your chin
and your chest, the four perfect chambers
of your heart, as you strain and strain
against the barrier I am.

Endometrial Biopsy

All this time, the pain
of your leaving
lodged in my tissues
like a landmine.

Today, tripped
by the doctor's needle,
it imploded
in concussive waves.

Afterward, weeping,
waiting to numb up
in the humiliation
of the stirrups,

I remembered our trip
to Planned Parenthood.
Having not *deflowered* me,
but rather

opened me, petal by petal,
to the goodness to come—
you held my hand for the exam.
When I was fully splayed,

the doctor asked
did you want to see,
and you took one look
at the place where possibility

would one day enter
and reality come squalling out,
and fainted away.
She rushed to bring you back,

while I lay cranked wide
on the table, the flushed, blank face
of my cervix, staring.
Smelling salts brought you

right around, but you never
really returned,
enlisting a few weeks later,
leaving me waiting

twenty-three years to find
what grief implanted
in my body's hushed,
brooding corridors.

Going to the Sperm Bank

Controversy whispered and blustered behind her.
The child won't know its father, they warned.

But she didn't listen.

Its medical history will lie, tangled and invisible,
until its roots finally breach the path.

                    She just smiled

when they suggested she photograph the paternal
test tube, commit to video the conception,
her feet firm in the stirrups, destiny bearing down
on her like desire.

The morning her temperature was right, she dressed
by candlelight, played love songs en route to the doctor
who waited, dressed white as a bride.

She didn't worry,
even when her abdomen grew furious with life.

But the words were there, disturbing the air around her.

What if the child is female and grows up beautiful,

as open as lilies they'll send with tentative
congratulations on her birth?

What if she develops a taste for older men?

Suppose she meets the donor, generous as cloudy weather,
eyes blue as her own—suppose, just suppose, he enters her,
stiff as that afternoon at the bank,

and sends sperm swimming upward, upward
to a place that finally looks like home.

Right to Life

It's like hiring a hitman.

—Pope Francis on abortion

I know what you are,
     little hitman, little cherub,

snuck up into me,
     swum past my barriers,

implanting like a movie monster who
     takes a person hostage from the inside.

You merely tap your unformed foot,
     and my body bursts into symphony,

blood volume cranked dizzyingly up,
     breasts swelling in fiery crescendo.

Nausea slams me forward,
     just as your father liked me:

a body bent double to take him.
     I'm on my knees, little one, surrendered,

vomit heaving out of me like prayers.
     I know, O, I know the life you've come for.

After

Once the body
was wrenched whole
from my body

I deflated
sank back into being
ordinary

a vessel
returned purposeless
to its shelf

I hadn't known
until first
the father

and then the son
swelled to fill
my emptiness

that I was
a space
a lack

that walked
through the world
or danced

or rested hollow
swinging her legs
on the future's sill

II

Proofs

When the Holy Spirit entered her, Mary was a room made dark
by the first sliver of light. Once void, she remained ever after
devoid of:

> the empty that exists when something has been taken away.

No woman who had lain after fullness and felt love trickle out of her
would have said, *Let it be done to me according to your word.*

Had she felt life unfurl inside her, or a child tear its way out, and then waited,
a wide wound, as her body closed, she would never have said,

*Give me the child already nailed into place, destined to run with the scissors of His life
pointed up. Let Him breach like a great whale beneath the dome of my stretched-taut
skin and force His way out of this slit husk. Behold.*

I am the handmaid of the Lord, His strange carapace.

The useless shell that cannot save Him.

Girlfriend of Las Vegas Gunman Says
Her Fingerprints Would Likely Be on Ammo

When it was hard for him
    to sleep
she matched her breath to his
    then waited
while they arced together
    into night's grave,
consciousness like a shot
    pulled beneath
the line of its trajectory
    by the force
no one can see. Those stale
    Sundays they ended
up at the range with a bag
    of guns
lugged in heavy from the car.
    The open air
always did them good, and there
    was something
intimate in seeing him
    take aim.
He always bested everyone,
    tore up the place.
After, she did her small part
    while they watched
news of other people's
    cataclysms.
Ammunition wedged warm
    between them
on the couch, they loaded
    the magazines.
Each elegant bullet
    was powerless

without its weapon.
      Like a woman
with no man to see her.
      Sometimes,
she wants him back.
      He touched her
the way she touched
      those bodies.
Her fingerprints
      entering them
on every round,
      his love
lodged inside her
      like a ghost.

Conduction

The man drives as closely to my car
as he can without making contact.
His truck window is down.
He is taking my right of way,
and I'm driving home, already crying,
from the audiologist's office.
I've turned the music on
and have just been thinking
that somewhere in Denmark,
an engineer lays her head
on a pillow filled, perhaps,
with eiderdown, her mind stuffed
with equations she mastered
in order to write the code
for the music setting on my
new hearing aids. They cost me
as much as a used car
and will not stop my nerves
from dying, cannot rebuild
this foundation that gradually
crumbles, but they have
resurrected, for this moment,
the voice of the trumpet
and polished its bright tones.
I cannot conceive of how
the years she bent to
her math books resulted
in this flashing beauty,
but I lean on it
the way a person leans
on a crutch when her knee
has given out, the way
I lean on Telemann who wrote
this concerto almost three hundred years ago,

each note big enough
to compensate, across time, for loss,
for the man passing slowly by,
menace blaring from his eyes,
as, triumphant, he raises
his middle finger like a baton.

Burdens

Already my daughter's looks
are something to bear.
Gold hair heavy
on her small shoulders.
Eyes big as burdens.

She can't escape
people looking at her,
so lets bangs grow
over her face
like thick curtains
almost closed.

Once, on the street,
a man touched
the glowing tip
of his cigarette
right to the center
of her forehead.

A crazy man, you say.
But I know
it was beauty
leaving its hot kiss.

Just Like All the Girls

I always knew

a man waited for me somewhere
with hands that fit the particular curves
of my treacherous body.

Whether I watched for him or not.
Whether I believed.

Sometimes, in dreams, he entered me from above,
like a coffin lowered slowly into a grave.

Sometimes he held me hard from behind.

The hills scorched golden each summer.
My hair was streaked the color of dried-dead grass.

People said I was lucky to have it.

Every year, moths fluttered
against the trees' dark trunks as I passed,
like scraps of parchment.

An infestation that maybe would, maybe would not, kill the oaks.

I dared myself to wonder
around which bend
would he find me.

Wherever I looked were signs.

The steep ridge, a gray fox hunting
at the slough's edge, *V* of geese going over.

World of enchantment,
and I wandered precarious,

my steps disturbing the air,
their small sound like beads
counting out prayers.

Trip-trap, my feet carried me along.

Almost to where he stood.
Expected. Unexpected.

Waiting that day in shadow,
white towel obscuring his face
like a veil.

His satchel was slung, open, over one shoulder.
It was yellow, the color of caution.

Every girl, I thought, has a man like that.

Pacing her ledges with his bag of tricks.
Readying himself
for her arrival.

His hands were sheathed
in royal blue Latex.

Like a doctor prepared for a procedure.

By the time I saw him,
he was so familiar
I almost forgot to run.

Rape Kit	Rape Kit
instructions	latex gloves
labels and forms	balaclava
evidence collection bags	trash bags
self-sealing envelopes	duct tape
vulvar/penile swabs	scissors
vaginal/cervical swabs	condoms
perianal/anal swabs	lubricant
sample containers	rope
blood collection supplies	knives
drug testing supplies	roofies
glass slides	pillowcase
nail scraper	handcuffs
comb	collapsible shovel
white sheets	tarp

All We Know

the gun was a   ghost
gun its parts   disparate
untraceable   as the boy's
path from son   friend and
athlete to shooter   when
first responders   arrived
it lay nearby   empty
as the boy   who was
bleeding   among the
rest of the   victims

Intention Tremor

My dog's neurology is unraveling.

He pushes his forehead to the precise place
my tibia juts almost through the skin,
where it feels like a shard,

and rests against that sharpness
as if wondering, *what the fuck*,

his brand new tremor rendering
everything unfamiliar
except my shin
where he returns,
again and again.

My life has skittered away from me, too,

like a ball of yarn, painstakingly shaped
from the raw skein, now sent spinning
across the world's slanting-away surface.

The dog whines, and I touch his head.

He can't negotiate
his water bowl anymore,
the clear liquid
in its usual container
flummoxes him,

just as I can't navigate to a life of *before*
and keep falling face-flat against *after*.

It's just *after after after* for the dog and me

as some higher power bats at us like a cat,
claws unsheathed, defenseless
in the presence of what creeps, unable to help
but take part in an unwinding.

As the dog cannot help but collapse
after he trembles, and I cannot help but pray,
bumping my skull against an edge
that feels broken.

As my girl cannot help but morph, like the dog,
something growing or withering in his head,
an illness spreading its dark wings in hers,

nothing we can see, no, but a presence
leering, indelible.

Like God.

Mistakes of One Kind

The dog was sleek, brindled.

He couldn't help people
wanting to touch him.

The silence of the beautiful is easy
to misconstrue.

I offered first my hand, then my face.

What's very large
is often hard to see.

His menace was like that.

What happens fast
can only be experienced
in retrospect.

His bite was like that.

I leaned into peril. Sweetly.
As if into a kiss.

I was always like that.

My face was sleek.
It caused its usual commotion.

The dog was brindled,
big as a man.

Once more, I was almost lucky.

A surgeon can revise
what a wound has written,
amend the story a dog's teeth made.

But I prefer to see my judgment
lapsed, then risen on my face.

The Dentist Says It's
from Some Earlier Damage

In my head, a dead tooth
is lodged among the living
as I am lodged in this life.

How can I tell
one thing
from another?

How can I explain I feel
like the tooth feels
now that it doesn't?

Dead or alive,
it gleams
in every picture,

only faintly discolored.
I appear smiling
in every moment

at the center of the family
while I house
some real thing

in a state of slow decay.
The pulp in my tooth
has nearly calcified

as I have nearly hardened
before the stove,
fixed, fastened,

a dead thing
no one realized
was dying.

I carry this tooth
in my mouth,
like a sentence

I cannot speak.

What Did I Know

By fourteen, I had lost
all patience with her
careful makeup, the fact
that she ate cattle, and swine,
and poultry, and said,
when asked, that she would
gladly *kill* anyone
who tried to hurt me.
She shaved her legs
and had not read
The Diaries of Anaïs Nin,
or *Johnny Got His Gun*,
or "The Ballad of the Lonely
Masturbator," failings
I ticked off silently
in the car beside her
those afternoons she drove me
to the orthodontist
she could not afford
so he could close the gaps
in my mouth, coax
my eye teeth from their
Count Dracula positions,
and give me, finally, the smile
that would oil the hinges
on so many of the world's doors.

She cleaned up after
construction workers to pay
for it, paint thinner
stripping her skin raw
when she used it to clean spatters
from the windows.
For two years, my mouth

ate up what might have gone
for her to have new shoes
or her own dentist.
When her tooth abscessed,
she waited it out,
swollen and hunched
in our kitchen,
a woman pummeled
by her love.

Containment

When the man sat down next to me at Starbucks, need coming off him like a pheromone, I was quiet, having read, more than once, *God save me from the well-meaning white woman,* for he was a person of color—I couldn't know which color, but not a *fucking white person* like me— and maybe I was *profiling* him, maybe I was an asshole and had already offended the Black woman who said I could share the table but packed up her things when I sat down, leaving me to chew my dry, multigrain bagel thoroughly like the stereotype it was and read an article about wildfires in Canada and how people watched their homes burn, at a comfortable distance, on cameras linked to their phones, until the man asked quietly, from his place to my side, if I could buy him a cup of coffee, his face open the way a wound is open, soft face about the age of my soft-faced son, and it was Mother's Day, and I couldn't escape the bounds of my whiteness, but I worried he was hungry, my son is always hungry, so I said I'd like to buy him something to eat, too, and asked was he okay, and he said he was, but life is strange right now, and I said, yes, isn't that the truth, and I had an appointment to get to and handed him twenty dollars from the stack in my purse and heard him order coffee and his bagel with cream cheese, and the Black woman came back and sat down as I walked out, my tears overflowing like clichés.

Dusk, the Day I Drove My Child to the Partial Hospitalization Program

The trees' branched openwork is bare, exposed
by autumn's fretsaw. Color shines through
the blank spaces, color of days closing like doors,
one by one, against me.

I pause, having emptied *properly* my little bucket
of food scraps, and wheeled the trashcans, relieved
of their stinking loads, back into place, snug
against our house.

I think of how succulents compost their own bodies, hold water
in each thick leaf, sit tidy in pots I've placed carefully on my
clean-swept porch. And did I tell you how useless it all is
before the ravages

of the starved synapse? Even the bread I bake doesn't help,
despite its wild rising, its very fine crumb.
Orchids on their bright sill, reliable, open
their freckled faces.

No small feat, this reblooming, when too much care
is as dooming as too little. I do everything meticulously,
walk motherhood's narrow ledge, and still stand
watching light fade

through the oaks' snarled tracery, watching it wane as the sky goes
from rose to pink to pale. It ends up black no matter,
the trees' outlines engulfed each night
by the dark.

Menopause, Insomnia, News

I flare up and die back down
        like the tip of God's cigarette
glowing in the difficult dark
        after a day spent running the world
into the ground. Aleppo, left out
        of the cease-fire, blazes,
and Prince overdosed in his elevator,
        unable to rise
above the sear of his pain.
        Three-year-old twins, untended,
roasted their baby sister in the oven,
        and I turn in my bed, dripping
like a pig on a spit, and think of my son
        who fell into a ring
of literal fire. In photographs,
        his palm smoldered,
a handful of embers. I wept, 1,013 miles away,
        when he called, alone
in his dorm, hopped up on morphine and afraid.
        When I was ten,
I touched the stove's element to see if it was hot.
        My two fingers, scorched
as a good steak. The worst part of any burn
        is the cold—
shivering while what remains chills
        like ashes, flicked onto snow.

Preferred Pronouns: We/Us/Ours

In the name of accuracy and inclusion

In the name of full disclosure

That we may say we love us and also that we hate us and be completely forthcoming

That we may wear the face of our beloved

That we may take up the first stone and smash that face to pulp

That we may be 100 percent right in our thinking and 100 percent wrong in our thinking 100 percent of the time

That to know us may make bile rise in our throats

That to know us may make delight bubble up into laughter

That, in our mirror, a moon glows golden

That, in our mirror, a cesspool glowers back

That whatever befalls one of us befalls all of us

That whatever we do to one of us we do to us all

That we see we are the dumpster fire we encircle to warm our greedy hands in the dark

III

Sorrow Is Innate in the Human

How new the child is.

Her cheeks with the look
of crisp apples,

but so soft they seem to melt
to my touch.

How little she has known
in her four-week life.

How short her hunger,
tethered to my breast,

pain limited to
inoculation's needle jab,

and even that
faced with the nipple
firm in her mouth.

Yet she knew enough
from the first to wake crying,

and for a terrible moment—inconsolable.

So long her journey
from my dreams
to my body to my arms.

So human the burden of grief
she brought with her.

What Small Sound

In the audiologist's booth, I clutch the device with the button
I'm to press if I hear a tone, hand clammy, the way
a child holds the finger of an adult she thinks can save her.

Behind the one-way glass, my ears are cupped in the pinching
headset, cilia becalmed, the quiet so thick I cannot stop
myself from thinking of Jupiter, its plentiful moons

I'm afraid to look at through the telescope, the stillness out there strong
enough to suck me in. What small sound might those moons make,
spinning in their vacuum, while I sit for what I know is too long

between tones? I'm here to bear witness to this deafness
that expands imperceptibly, the way the universe, they say,
is expanding even as my world narrows, sound swirling round the drain

of this loss. Into the silence of the audiologist's booth
fall consonants, vowels, rain against my windows, my lover's voice
disappearing like a star's light being swallowed and swallowed as it dies.

Like a Friend

You are hung safely in the past now,
fixed in the frame of the photograph
from that day in the mountains when I was afraid
but you went right in, trusting your body
to the body of the lake, its coldness
that held you even as the bottom dropped
away. I'd like to remember you
floating in the green world
of the water, the heavens broken open
like a vault above us, and summer
pouring through. How you waved
from the other side, elegant and straight,
slender as an exclamation point.
Last week, after life curdled
inside you, like milk gone slowly,
irrevocably sour, they found you
suspended in the dark of the winter park.
I'd like to imagine you peaceful,
your fall caught by a snare you shaped
yourself, pausing a moment between one world
and the next, feet lightly brushing
the ground, your body a shore
you'd already pushed off from.
I'd like to think of your hair shining
white as bone in the moonlight
as the tree stood unbending
in its mercy, and the end of your life
rushed up, like a friend, to greet you.

Love Is a Song You Listen to Later

Reading about whales—captive beluga who tried to learn to talk, blue whales calling to each other across entire oceans—I think how like that beluga I was, my adolescence spent trying to decrypt isolation.

If you played my efforts back, the way they play back the beluga's recordings, there would be a haunting gibberish, something that sounds like speech but carries no meaning.

At seventeen, when I met the boy, I was a strange white whale behind aquarium glass, my face pressed to transparent confinement, a sadness eddying and sinking.

Slowly, mouth to mouth, he made me human.

Sounds we shared became words, language, an incantation.

It's years since he left my solitude for his bright-lit life, but I hear him from across time's littered floor when I slide, again, into a darkness so complete I needn't bother having eyes.

His voice still the hand on my elbow in the room of strangers.

Swimming the Flambeau

A man pulled an albino musky
from the Flambeau River today.
An undeserving man, I know,
for he held her up, her shining body
a torch against his darkness,
and took her measure, smiling
for the newspaper photograph
while the air poisoned her
and the brightness began to burn.

Another man would have known
what it cost her to survive
to her great length and seen
she was as stark and obvious
as a beautiful woman—
unequipped for sunlight,
or the air's fingers scorching her gills,
or a man's hands rough
along her sleek sides.

This man would have dispensed entirely
with rod, reel, and hook barbed
as a clever line tossed casually
from a barstool. It would have sufficed
for him to lower his own bare body
into the Flambeau River and swim
up on her quietly, small hands glowing
as his tapered fingers moved softly
through the cool, green water.

Why I Don't Drink

Because drink is a man with eyes more ocean than sky,

with wit, whose good humor surrounds him like fragrance,

whose suits sit just right and don't wrinkle,

who wants to pour himself into me

and brings me books—the right books—

and takes me to a hotel room above an exotic city,

and dresses me in silk just for the pleasure of sliding it down,

who enters me like a flush of good fortune—

who, it turns out, is married, and likes to hang me

over his knees and smack me till welts rise up burning,

and I spend a long time later, bent funny before a mirror,

straining to see the bruises on my backside,

wondering if this was a price I wanted to pay.

And by then, honey, it's too late.

Rhubarb

I.

Sometimes cooking is like being
with you. Uncovering each layer,
onions knife my eyes. I was a girl
watching you in the kitchen.
You taught me to peel back the delicate
skin, to make the pieces small.
Cooking, it's okay to cry
when life bubbles beneath your masked face,
bitter as rhubarb stewing on the stove.
Even sugar doesn't erase the taste
passed from your mouth to mine.

II.

Peeling peaches, I remember
your slight weight against the edge
of sink and think, if you had moved,
the house would have fallen
around us. My own sink
is cool now, hard against the hollow
my hips make. Peach skins gash
its white surface. Divided, bare,
the fruit smells like you.
I see the darkness of each half
bleeding out from the center.

Sometimes My Face Flushes
When I Make Love

I won't make love in the closet
even if you're gentle
between suitcoats and dress shirts.

I prefer light trickled across bedsheets
and the door locked.

I remember the stained carpet—
Satan's footsteps, we thought—
outside the closet where my sister found us,

neighbor boy and I, four years old, with our pants down,
pale globes of our buttocks shining in the dark.

Mother, in the kitchen, slicing
peaches and making Jell-O salad for dinner
with her friends and their mean children, stopped:

I, no matter my braids and big eyes,
was to be grounded for a week.

I stood, little arms unfolded and my fingers, just the tips, tingling.

So shame began without precision,
just a wash of color across my face.

Mother said she wouldn't tell
the daughters, the one son whose name was Rusty.
Rusty like cans, like the rumps of ponies.

But I remember my hot cheeks.

The Jell-O tasted of berries and laughter.
And peaches, stark in their bowl,
sat all juicy without their skins.

How Like a God

Making tiny work
of what I could not budge,
the bear lifted my left-out cooler—so heavy

it would have taken two people
to stagger it to safety—
and slammed it down, snapping its hinges.

I lay in my flimsy shelter as he tore into
what he wanted, smacked his lips,
snuffled loudly for blueberries.

Such fondness for small pleasures
within that shouldered broadness.
What he liked, he licked carefully the last of

then left my ice chest strewn,
jagged valleys notched in its surface,
useless latch like a mouth, hung open.

Two days later, you were hospitalized.
My pain was tented, silent. Night after night,
it lay inside the pitch black of me, listening

while your illness rummaged
inside you, digging, clawing,
sniffing for the sweetest parts.

Admissions

I bring retainers
to hold her teeth in situ
while the rest of her slips askew,

and a change of clothes
though all the days she's here
I know she will not change,

and three kinds of floss
which they won't give her
because: hanging.

The nurses turn their backs
to this locked ward,
bored with suffering.

Merciless, this hospital
where I lay
and forced her out

and the years since,
trying to live
in the suffocating space

between our rock
and our allotted
hard place.

The Way Some People Laugh at Funerals

When he hasn't come   after me

after all and I've run   all the way home

and he's not   given chase

I can't help chuckling   in the safety of my hallway

to imagine him   his long sleeves and pants

Latex pulled tight as skin   over his hands

towel on his head   under his hat

bag like a workman's   slung over

one shoulder   wondering how long

he crouched in the heat waiting   for me

where the trees thicken   at the ridge top

all dressed up   and no one to do

One Day, My Body

I'm tethered
since the man
on the ridge,

limited to the path
between the backyards
and the cemetery.

This body is a rope
that swings me
over want's abyss.

I am weak, succulent,
a magnet for men
who hide in the woods.

I knew that trail
like the ridges of
my own body

that rose up
and changed
everything.

It was my ridge,
the way once
it was my body,

when I was
lanky-straight
and invisible,

before possibility
unleashed itself,
month by month,

inside me. One day,
there was a stranger
on the trail

as one day,
my body curved
out of control

making men
do things
I regretted.

What makes a man
want a woman
dead

or pinned,
unmoving,
beneath him?

It's bright here
on the fire road
between gardens

and graves.
Vultures perch
on the chimneys,

wings spread
to the new day.
A deer's carcass rests

in the creek beyond
the chain link.
I am safe here

in the open
among the already
always deceased.

Lightning Coming Closer All the Time

I can't tell from here
if the Lord is a sniper
or a drunk guy with a shotgun.

Whether He's poised with His scalpel
and scrubs or just reaching into
His pickup for a hacksaw.

I see my neighbor, raising a girl
my daughter's age, check into the hospital
for kidney stones and come home

with stage IV lymphoma.
A friend's husband, twenty years her senior,
like mine, falls to a heart attack

with a one-way ticket to a nursing home
clutched in its fist. The boy from my son's school
lies in a coma after taking a baseball

at 100 mph to the head—his skull fractured
in precisely the place my son
was twice concussed.

Sometimes, I want to take my fist
to the face of God or duck my head,
but I keep still out here in the open,

humanity hung on me like a metal suit,
dread dripping off me like rain.

Breaking Eggs

I cry when I bake   since that boy   slugged you
repeatedly   in the head   knocking the numbers out
so you couldn't count to five   though you were
eight   and adding   was out of the question
you woke   after that   with a scream pitched high
as a rabbit's cry   after a rifle shot   you couldn't walk
down stairs anymore   without falling   and once you climbed
to the counter   where I found you   sweating   trying
to recall   how to get down   at first   you couldn't hear us
then suddenly   even a whisper was a shout   the volume
turned so loud   it seemed your head would burst
with sound   the doctor likened the head to an egg   skull
the hard shell protecting the fragile brain   brain the golden yolk
floating in its sturdy cage   that boy   he said   shook
the egg of you   until the yolk bounced   bruised   this morning
I hesitate   over each egg   struck   by the thought
of his fist   of his other hand   holding your arm
so you couldn't move   thinking of your head   so small
in the beginning   of the soft parts   it seemed
my finger   might go through

My Daughter Was Always the Resourceful One

In the days of her death wish, my eyes were fixed, open,

my life a watchtower I couldn't stop looking down from.

She couldn't be trusted even to sleep separately then

though we'd locked up so many things:

belts that seemed innocent before her

the well-meaning medicines

electrical cords in their tyranny of tangles

her scarves/my scarves

the noose we found when we searched her closet

two deluxe Swiss Army knives

a handful of bare blades she'd extracted from her plastic razors

all our shoelaces in a messy, little pile

dental floss, reeking of mint

keys to all four cars

and every pair of scissors in the house no matter how small.

I lay beside her in the dark to watch, weeping,

while she kept on breathing against her will.

I worked so hard to give her life.

She worked so hard to hand it back.

Lessons

My daughter dreads middle school science
      because all they study is cataclysm,
            end-stopped species after end-stopped species,
            earth's slow dwindling.
         There is no longer a world to study
    that teems with life, not a globe ecstatic
in its wild spinning. Day after day,
      they regard the crumbling edge,
            broken asphalt where a road runs out
               and we launch ourselves like lemmings
         over the side. When I was a girl,
    my most lasting science lesson consisted
of pinching pieces one by one from
      my mother's impatiens plants then watching
         through a tiny drinking glass as
            each stalk sent new roots fingering out
         into the water. My daughter sits quiet
    in science through all the bad news.
She sits quiet during the active shooter
      drills, even the one that goes on so long
         her teacher thinks it is the real thing,
            and she's quiet in the car after the birthday
         party for the girl whose mom was killed
    by that crazy man in Las Vegas. I tell her I want to go
solar, because of global warming, and she says
      she hates science, and I keep thinking
         of the IRS auditor we had—the one who truly regretted
            telling us what a shoddy bookkeeper I am—
      how he used to be a CPA and missed it.
    His clients all had futures back then,
and he helped to plan them.
      Being an IRS agent is all forensics
         the way eighth-grade science is all
            forensics now. The way when I think

of the future, it's more like looking
at an ending than a beginning. Like
        performing an autopsy on something
                though it keeps on living. At dinner,
                        my daughter reminds me she hates
                vegetables, says I should let her
        eat whatever she wants to now, while
she's young and still can. Looking
        backward at her future, I think
                she may be right. Maybe it already
                        will not matter.

IV

Where We Are Most Tender

Mostly love is about grunt work,
heaving unwieldy pieces of furniture
up a trackless mountain,
the heat and humidity punishing,
mosquitoes ravenous. They bite
where we are most tender
and can't slap with our full hands.

We love with our restraint, lying
silent through bitter nights,
doing the left-foot right-foot trudge
of resentment:
our hearts like Indian guides
leading stupid white settlers
into wilderness.

They don't even turn
to check if we're there—
they know we'll follow.

Taking Your Place

After they locked you in the famous hospital,
I scoured your shut-up rooms
on my hands and knees.

Nights, I lay on your bathroom floor,
tiles gleaming in the dark,
your mad clutter cleared away.

You'd read online it's possible
to hang yourself without leaving
the ground, brought a pillow for your head,

a comfort measure. I tried to fit my body where
I would have found yours,
slender neck belted with the leather strap.

When the nurses didn't watch you
overnight, I called the hospital
to complain. The director sighed

and spoke slowly, as to a dim child.
You know, he said, *a determined person* will *kill
herself no matter what we do.*

Since they sent you home, I keep on checking.
Is the laundry dry? Do we need more sugar?
Are you alive?

Day by day, I creep, pain-scuttled,
laid flat as by a deer who's crushed
her shape permanently into grass.

I've learned to wait.
But, though you returned,
I do not think I'm coming back.

Late Mammogram

Standing before the newest-fangled
3D machine I open my gown to the tech
who leads me by my right breast
into position, cheerful but not particularly
kind, her job requiring a dedicated
sternness, the willingness to grab
what is private and lay it out
on the clear plastic breast tray
and really have a look,
her repeated instructions: *Do not*
raise your shoulders, keep both
feet on the floor, lean in,
and then the flattening
of the stretched-out tissues
until I just cross the border
into pain and hold myself there,
face jutting out at a weird angle
so as not to be in the way,
while the machine murmurs,
considering me as it travels
its slow arc, and the tech
instructs me periodically to
stop breathing, and it feels familiar
to hold the unnatural pose
and my breath simultaneously,
and I get to thinking about nursing,
how these tired slabs of flesh
once swelled with milk, grew
spherical as planets
with each child's days revolving
around them, which reminds me
of Mars and the rover sent off
to take pictures of what we
cannot reach, the way this

machine makes an image
of what we cannot see, and I feel
my life slowly draining the life
from me the way we siphon everything
from this planet that once was
teeming as my breasts that day
my milk came in and shot
across the room in two narrow arcs,
and the tech tells me to step away
and breathe freely, then reaches
for my second breast and deposits it,
depleted, on the tray, and that rover failed
to solve any of our problems
though this mammogram may identify
one of mine, and as the tech shoves
and smashes me into place I
remember the tracks the rover left,
solitary in the red dust, as she went forth
and discovered there's really nothing
there to save us, which puts me in mind
of Barbara's biopsy and Hanna's and Lyn's,
their breasts become biohazard,
and I consider the biological hazards
of the years to come, and then
the machine whirs again, and once,
I read, the rover was stuck
in a dune more than a month,
and wind blew sand onto her batteries
blocking the sun but blew it back off,
and my ribs hurt and my breast,
and even the insects
are on the brink, and this week,
they declared the Mars rover dead
which makes me think of the photo

of the emaciated polar bear
on his patchy ice and the one of the girl
slowly starving in Yemen, and I
wonder why I'm trying so hard
to stay alive, and, *stop breathing*,
says the tech, and I know
my battery is low
and it's getting dark.

Scorpions

Scorpions have such big hearts,
my daughter tells me, pointing
to the diagram in her book.
Every winter, we gather them in glass jars.
My girl likes their utter
stillness, the way they rest harmless
until provoked. She is quiet, so fragile
she misses school some days
because she wakes crying and cannot stop.
Her brother teases her, his voice
sharp as the end of a stick.
Her anger is quick when she turns it on him
as the sudden whip when the scorpion
curls its tail over. The fat, venom tip
swaying just above the great heart.

The Sound When the Held Note Ceases

Tonight I contemplate, thirty years late,
his dark head cradled in my lap,
teenage boy from band snuck back with me
to our grade-school playground,
middle of a bitter night,
and him telling me he'd been adopted
twice, and me considering the mother
who gave him up, one who died
when he was two, and finally one who lasted,
her voice cool when I'd called
for him that afternoon.

We sat cross-legged in the cold
as he pulled open the heavy doors
of my coat and made quick work
of my buttons, solving easily
the puzzle of the front clasp
on my bra. He sighed to see
my breasts spring free,
pale and rising in the frigid air—
then leaned across my lap
and settled in, my arms around him,
his body stretched upon the frozen ground.

His lips grazed one nipple
before enveloping it, as I'd watched him hold
each woodwind he prepared to play.
When he began to suck,
his eyes slid shut, one hand slack
above my heart.
Other mouths had touched me there,
but none ever pulled this sweetness up.
It welled in me like sorrow, or satiety,
like tears one almost weeps.

So far beyond desire—I nursed him
in the moonlit schoolyard and felt a hollowing
hunger I couldn't name, a wistful, tender longing
even thirty years would fail to slake.
I held him, rocking a little, as we fell
through the ravenous, murmuring dark
of our separate aches.

Becoming

Once, I was a whole person.
I agreed to be transformed,
through trauma, into pieces.
I laid myself cheerfully down
before the apocalypse.
After, the doctor placed the baby
among my body's wreckage.
I learned to call this *love*.

Tutor

I required, finally, a boy with twelve years
of piano lessons singing in his hands,
and the girlfriend before me who taught him
to play scales up and down her body.
He reached casually between my legs,
without needing to look,

to place one practiced finger on my clitoris
and press as if freeing a clear note from his piano.
My body did the rest, bucking against him,
then arching with an involuntary, jubilant moan.
I lay after, amazed and chagrined to think of pleasure,
a spring coiled all that time in my body.

Hush

Evenings, sick of acuity
       and its cost,
I pull at my hearing aids
       until what entered
each ear slides slowly out,
       drawing sound
along with it, deafness a relief
       as when I've had
all I can take of pleasure
       and push my lover
from my body. The world,
       it's true, is less
absent the part of him
       that fills and empties me
at once, ecstasy an overwhelm
       like life's din
played by the devices in my head,
       insistent music
I finally writhe away from.

Love in the Time of Covid-19

for my husband, twenty-one years my senior

There are so many times
I could have killed you.

After twenty-eight years of marriage—
the only contact sport
I've ever stuck with—

I found myself

crying this morning,
after a trip outside,
singing *Happy Birthday*

three times through,

just to be sure,

scrubbing despite
the sting of my split skin

as I've loved you
through even the rub
of the raw years.

I held my hands steady
in the water's reassuring scald,

trying and trying
to save you.

Turning a Corner

Five years into your child's illness,
when you can no longer conceive of life
without its dank presence, you see
a blanched sky bearing a trace of rose
and the moon, risen huge—
an affront like your lover's face
turned toward you for the last time,
his sweet, rescinded body a scaffold
you once clung to. Radiant in departure,
he gazed back, bright as this orb God raises
to say, *Look. This is what I can do.*
This is what I refuse to do for you.

How Destruction Comes to
Look Like Possibility

Today a contractor stood
in our family room,

tore down a small wall,
and pulled the fireplace out like a plug

to make way for a different angle,
a right angle, which will allow

for a new wall to push your piano
up against, instrument we bought

when you came home
from the locked ward

where you taught yourself to play
"Für Elise" one slow note at a time,

and I stood quietly, peering
into the unfamiliar emptiness,

as I had stood listening to you
through the phone

those months ago, leaning
into the pocket of air,

the strange openness
I didn't know to think existed,

beyond demolition, waiting
on the other side.

After the Hearing Test

it's two days before I cry.

Grief sneaks up on me
the way sound does now,

my ability to mourn as sluggish
as my inner ears.

Cilia do not rejuvenate.
We have that in common.

I won't mind losing the clamor
of cocktail parties,

high grind
of the dentist's drill,

triggering retch
of other people's vomit,

but I'd like to keep
Telemann's Trumpet Concerto in D;

the tiny chuff my python makes
up close to my ear;

the calls of two Canada geese
as they circled the slough this morning,

seeming lost, their cries trailing them
like a woman's heavy train;

and the indecipherable murmur
of my beloved's voice

as she held my hand while the bear
ate my baked beans just outside our tent.

Though I could not make out her assurances,
may they burble over me forever.

Loss accrues, the geese can tell you.
It compounds. Like interest.

Oh, world, leave me slowly.
Let me dally over each diminishing return.

Deciduous

I want to be the tree
when cold has come,

after rain has run like lovers' fingers
down my thick body,

and my leaves
have burst into burning.

I want to glow like embers
that are the fire dying,

burning hotter and hotter
until it's gone.

I want my branching
darkness exposed

by the transparent insistence
of wind

as it pulls, piece by piece,
my bright raiment off.

I want to feel what's next
curled inside me, tight as fists.

Perimenopause

Mornings now, I shave the dusky down
moustache from my upper lip.
My skin, unused to the razor's blading
glide, its scrape, breaks open
in tiny bumps. The way I'm casually broken
open all the time lately, my tears
unchanneled and at the smallest
provocation making glistening runnels
down cheeks that sprout a new meadow
of man-fuzz. Like the boys of my youth,
I gangle, awkward, trip over my own
altered self, my loins alight with a strange,
new life. Last week, in the produce aisle, a man
I've never been drawn to hugged me,
his hands warm the way a pilot light
is warm, its staid flicker merely dependable
in the dusty window of a hot water heater,
but I danced to life like a kerosene
slick touched by the sweet carelessness
of a match and stood there, helplessly burning.

Manifest Image

The man keeps telling me I'm beautiful.
I still look young.

He says it like I've asked for it,
but I don't care.

For him or beauty.

I am content to slip into old,
wrinkled plainness,

to walk on, unimpeded.

I was young once.
My body stunned.
My breasts were really something,

but I was something else entirely.

Something no one could see
until now.

Biographical Note

Francesca Bell is a poet and translator. Her debut collection, *Bright Stain* (Red Hen Press, 2019), was a finalist for the Washington State Book Award and the Julie Suk Award. Her work appears widely in magazines such as *ELLE*, *Los Angeles Review of Books*, and *Rattle*. Bell grew up in Washington and Idaho and did not complete middle school, high school, or college. She is the translation editor of the *Los Angeles Review* and lives with her family in Novato, CA.